Praise

"Mark Hansen hit a home run for teens in his dollars and sense approach to achieving financial success. This book is a must read with incredible value."
~Jeff Atwater, Chief Financial Officer, State of Florida

"Mark Hansen has the prescription for teens to win financially. If we could distribute this book to every teenager in America, we would all be enriched. Hansen is a great financial guru for those emerging into adulthood. I gave the book to my own daughter, the minute I was done reading it!"
~Keith Ablow, M.D., Psychiatrist, NY Times Bestselling Author and Fox News Contributor

"The attributes touched upon in Hansen's new book—saving, giving, budgeting, planning, learning, and goal setting—provide a solid framework for building young entrepreneurs. This book is filled with content and spells out the 'how-to' for teens to be successful."
~Dr. Nido R. Qubein, President, High Point University, Chairman of the Great Harvest Bread Company

"This easy-to-understand book lays out in simple terms a sound approach to managing money and creating wealth. I am buying it for all my teenagers."
~Charles P. Garcia, best-selling author of *Leadership: Lessons of the White House Fellows* and *A Message from Garcia*

"Think about it. Where do our kids get their financial literacy—the TV? In school? Really, neither, until it is too late—if ever. Well, Mark Hansen changes everything with his new book. Hansen teach

they need to learn—early! Schools across the country should make this book required reading."

~Frank McKinney, best selling author, *The Tap* and *Make it Big! 49 Secrets for Building a Life of Extreme Success*

"Once again, Hansen hits the mark with his passion and effectiveness for empowering and inspiring teens. It's about time we began educating our youth to become financially successful and responsible. This book is packed with simple easy to follow ideas and principles that teens can put into action today!"

~Allen West, U.S. Congress

"Finally, a book to teach teens how to handle their money through simple common sense guidelines."

~Dennis P. Gallon, Ph.D., President, Palm Beach State College

"Mark's book is a helpful tool for any teenager or parent to bridge the gap from the teenage years to adulthood. You have a must read book here—it is informative and practical. This book is loaded with the tools and answers it takes to be a huge success in today's marketplace."

~Omar Periu, best-selling author, CEO of Omar Periu International

"Mark Hansen has written a book that can set young people on the path to successful, productive, happy lives. We are very proud that he is a graduate of Florida Atlantic University."

~Mary Jane Saunders, Ph.,D., President, Florida Atlantic University

"Education is key! Why don't our schools teach our younger generations to become financially literate? If this was required for ALL teens, we wouldn't be in the financial position we are in now. This is a must read for every teenager out there! As we know, the one area in life that every single person eventually has to deal with is money. It is about time there is a book that will provide a road map...a blue print for our teens to become financially successful."

"An invaluable book to teach teens how to spend wisely, save wisely, give wisely, and most importantly, feel empowered by their own financial decisions, both now and in the future. A must-read for all teens, and a great refresher course for adults who may be reeling from today's economic climate."

SUCCESS 101 FOR TEENS

DOLLARS AND $ENSE FOR A WINNING FINANCIAL LIFE

SUCCESS 101 FOR TEENS

DOLLARS AND $ENSE FOR A WINNING FINANCIAL LIFE

by Mark Hansen
with Kevin Ferber

PARAGON HOUSE

Published in the United States by
Paragon House
1925 Oakcrest Avenue, Ste 7
St. Paul, MN 55113-2619

Special thanks to Michael Brown for his contribution to Cutcaster
"Helping hand to pie chart business financial success" used on cover.

First e-book, 2012
e-book ISBN: 978-1-61083-059-1

Library of Congress Cataloging-in-Publication Data

Hansen, Mark, 1968-
 Success 101 for teens : dollars and sense for a winning financial life / by Mark Hansen ; with Kevin Ferber. -- 1st ed.
   p. cm.
 Summary: "Teaches teens basic principles of financial management, planning, and success; includes questions, exercises, and forms that lead to
the creation of a financial plan by the reader upon completion of the book"--Provided by publisher.
 ISBN 978-1-55778-901-3 (pbk. : alk. paper)
 1. Finance, Personal--Juvenile literature. 2. Success--Psychological aspects. 3. Teenagers--Life skills guides. I. Ferber, Kevin S., 1969- II. Title. III. Title: Success one-oh-one for teens. IV. Title: Success one hundred one for teens.
 HG179.H257 2012
 332.02400835--dc23
          2011048099

The paper used in this publication meets the minimum requirements of American National Standard for Information—Permanence of Paper for Printed Library Materials, ANSI Z39.48-1984.

Manufactured in the United States of America

10 9 8 7 6 5 4 3 2 1

For current information about all releases from Paragon House, visit the web site at

www.ParagonHouse.com

www.success101forteens.com

Dedication

This book is dedicated to young people, with the hope that they develop these dollar and sense habits within themselves and the fruits gained from them in the successes in their own lives.

Watch your pennies and your dollars will take care of themselves. ~Benjamin Franklin

Acknowledgments

We would like to thank all of our friends and family for being there for us over the years and for the support that you have given us for our work. For their continued encouragement to write another book in the *Success 101* series, we want to thank our team at Paragon House and especially Rosemary and Gordon for their confidence in us. Our wonderful editor Erica Orloff has given us tremendous guidance and wisdom. A special thank you to Meril Stumberger and Margaret Cohen for their continued inspiration. Lastly, we want to recognize Mark's wife, Jane, and Kevin's wife, Pam, for their unconditional support and love.

CONTENTS

Chapter Seven

Chapter Eight

Part II

Foreword

As I watch my son, Colby John, play flag football—charging up and down the field without a care in the world—I marvel at how quickly he is growing up. Soon enough, like so many parents, my wife and I will have a full-grown teenager living among us. And, let me just say it is a sobering thought for so many reasons.

Teens and dollars and sense. That will be, no doubt, the topic of one of numerous thorny conversations my son and I will have in the coming years. To further complicate matters, he is growing up at a time of global economic distress. There are families who have lost their homes to foreclosure, businesses that have collapsed, and people whose life savings have evaporated because of fluctuations in the stock market. How can we ensure that generations to come are prepared to meet future economic challenges?

It starts with financial literacy. As a lifelong educator, I am amazed how little attention is given to teaching students how to handle personal finances. Ultimately, our schools, universities and communities will benefit from a citizenry that learned how to make good decisions about money at an early age. As a nation and as a global community, we have the responsibility to teach these concepts to every single person before they set out on their own.

Success 101 for Teens: Dollars and Sense for a Winning Financial Life lays out the plain-language wisdom of creating a six-step life game-plan focused on saving, giving, budgeting, planning, learning, and goal setting in order to create a lifestyle of sound financial strength in their futures.

Mark Hansen is a remarkable person who has used a traumatic, life-altering childhood experience as an example to others of what's possible even when others tell you that you can't. As a young child, he was struck by a car and suffered a serious brain injury. Mark overcame paralysis, seizures, delays in schooling, and continuous bullying from others throughout his childhood and understands the challenges and pressures that teens endure. It is because of these experiences that Mark is passionate about helping youth.

The teen years can be hard enough, so anything that makes life a little easier is worthwhile. This book is an invaluable "how to" guide for financial literacy, which can help your child make smart decisions now that will have a lasting impact for years to come.

Frank T. Brogan, Chancellor of the State University System of Florida.

Chapter One

Introduction: Success 101

What's success?

In writing this book, I found all sorts of ways to define success. There's the dictionary way. The dictionary says success is a noun meaning, "Achieving something planned or attempted."

I intended to get up and write a chapter today. If I finish this chapter I'm writing, then I've had success. In fact, I successfully brewed my coffee today—I was successful at it. (Thank goodness!) But my definition of success goes a bit deeper than that.

A random Google search for "success quotes" will turn up 35,000,000+ entries. That's a huge number of ways to define success, don't you think? Here are some of my favorites.

❖ "Success doesn't come to you . . . you go to it." ~Marva Collins

❖ "Real success is finding your lifework in the work that you love." ~David McCullough

❖ "Success is more permanent when you

achieve it without destroying your principles."
~Walter Cronkite

❖ "The person who gets the farthest is gen-
erally the one who is willing to do and dare.
The sure-thing boat never gets far from shore."
~Dale Carnegie

❖ "Many of life's failures are people who did
not realize how close they were to success when
they gave up."~Thomas Edison

❖ "Always bear in mind that your own reso-
lution to succeed is more important than any
other."~Abraham Lincoln

❖ "The thing always happens that you really
believe in; and the belief in a thing makes it
happen."~Frank Lloyd Wright

❖ "The difference between a successful person
and others is not a lack of strength, not a lack
of knowledge, but rather a lack in will."~Vince
Lombardi

❖ "Success is to be measured not so much
by the position that one has reached in life
as by the obstacles which he has overcome."
~Booker T. Washington

Depending on what kind of person you are, or your values, being a success can be as simple as being a happy person. It can be as complicated as being head of a multinational corporation with assets in the billions. It can mean accomplishing a dream or a long-held wish to learn something or travel somewhere. You can have success in the sports arena, or in the educational arena. The thing about true success is that you define it.

As you define your vision of success, it is important to realize success has many facets—spiritual, emotional, relationship success, educational ... and financial. A very wealthy person is not successful, in my opinion, if he is a stingy, ungenerous person who is nasty to everyone in the office and makes life miserable for every person he encounters from the waiter at his usual restaurant to his employees to his family. *Money does not make you successful.*

However, having very little money and a great deal of financial stress can put a huge damper on how happy or successful a person feels. Think about it. You are crazy about some guy or girl and want to go to the prom. But you have no money, and Mom and Dad can't loan you any. It puts a damper on things. Or what about stressing about how you are going to pay for college? Or pay for gas for your car ... or even save up for a car? Look into the future. Money woes place great stresses on *families.* If you cannot afford to feed your family, or if you and your life partner fight about money all the time, then financial "success" is important to your happiness.

As I traveled all over for the book tour for my last Success 101 book, I met many people—teens and adults—very stressed out about money. In the years since I started writing my first book to today, the United States, and indeed the world, has experienced unprecedented (in my life and yours) economic difficulties. I met many teens on my book tour whose parents were in dire financial difficulties, and now college, something they had planned on, was not going to be immediately possible. Or now they would have to take out very large loans because their college funds no longer had the money in them that they once did.

I also met teens who had to help their parents financially. Some kids were working two or more part-time jobs, plus babysitting. I met teens who were literally in tears with stress because their family home had been foreclosed on and they were going to have to move—change schools and change their lives.

In addition, I met many teachers. I am proud of the work I have done over the years on behalf of educators and education. Twice I was elected to the School Board of Palm Beach County, the eleventh-largest school district in the entire United States. I know first hand the difficulties schools, students, and teachers have first-hand and the budget woes schools face. I have been on the front lines of education! I also speak regularly to schools and students as an author. It is one of my favorite things to do.

I know then, directly from teachers, that "financial illiteracy" is a big problem for teens. Many kids today don't know how to balance a checkbook. They don't really understand how interest rates and credit cards work. That scares me as a champion for youth today. Why? Because if you do not obtain a firm financial education, you can wind up in the same kinds of difficulties that many people are facing right now. It can hinder your future success—however you define it.

Whatever you want to accomplish, whatever profession you choose, whatever your goals are for a family or travel or career, I want you to be able to achieve it. I want every teen to be a success. As I look around at the financial situation of our country today, I know that the tools I am about to teach you in this book are tools you can use your entire life.

You can grow your own wealth—right here, right now. And even if you don't aspire to riches ... you can live your entire life debt-free, or at least very much in control of that debt.

So I hope you are excited to learn some new Success 101 principles. If you follow the steps and ideas in this book, you, too, will have a winning financial life!

* * * * *

TECH TALK

Each chapter will cover a financial strategy. Then, throughout the text, technology tools for teens will be set in Tech Talk boxes, utilizing the best the Web and technology has to offer young financial wizards. There is a glossary of financial terms in the back of the book. And in Part II of the book, there is a workbook for you to write down your financial goals, budget, and other things that you learn in this book.

www.success101forteens.com

Chapter Two

Traits and Strategies

What fundamental traits and strategies can create a winning financial approach? Believe it or not, the same elements for a successful adult financial picture are those for teens. I describe the Success 101 approach as:

- ❖ Saving
- ❖ Giving
- ❖ Budgeting
- ❖ Planning
- ❖ Learning
- ❖ Goal Setting

Let's examine each one in brief here.

Saving

If you've ever saved for a special purchase, or if you are saving your money for a big purchase like a car or special trip, then you already know what's involved with saving money. But there's much more to saving than simply sticking money in a jar in your bedroom. When we explore saving, you'll learn a variety of different strategies and learn how little savings can add up to giant rewards.

Giving

While some people my age and older seem to discourage teens, I think you are the most exciting people to be around: you're full of possibility and dreams and hopes. Every classroom I visit rewards me with unbridled optimism and energy! You're also a very generous bunch. Teens today are more engaged with societal issues than ever before. Whether it's living "green," caring about abandoned pets at the SPCA, church, or other religious organizations, or caring about any cause near to your hearts, this chapter will teach you both the importance of generosity and how to go about using your finances to help those causes important to you.

Budgeting

If you have ever taken some of your money and set it aside for a payment on a purchase or for different expenses in your life, then you have the start of a basic budget. But where, exactly, does your money go? If you have a part-time job or receive an allowance, how do you keep from spending every nickel you make the minute the money is in your hands? A budget can help you feel like you are in the driver's seat with your finances. It can also help you SAVE money. We'll cover that in the budgeting chapter!

Planning

Planning is a way to establish a vision. I don't know anyone who says they just want to "make do," or "get by." Most of us—especially teens—have passions and dreams and visions for the future. In this chapter, you will explore your financial vision. Once you know your vision, you can make plans to achieve it. Planning also helps you avoid the number-one nemesis on the way to financial success: impulse spending.

Learning

No, this is not about schoolwork. This is about your financial education. This country has a major problem: financial illiteracy. Many adults do not understand how credit works, how to avoid soul-crushing debt, and other financial disasters. As such, it's no wonder that most teens do not understand these concepts either. In addition, even some basic financial education—things like establishing a college fund, or balancing a checkbook—are a mystery to many teens. I'm here to help you understand a few basics about finances so you will have those tools for the rest of your life.

Goal Setting

Without goals—for everything from education to savings—teens (and adults) can feel like they are on a hamster's wheel, living from one paycheck or allowance to another. Goals help establish a winning "big picture" for a successful life. This chapter includes advice on saving and paying for college or trade school.

Entrepreneurship and Careers

Adults ask children what they want to be when they grow up almost from the moment kids can talk. This chapter explores the role a career or entrepreneurial venture can play in developing financial success. Some teen entrepreneurs make a fortune while still too young to vote! Turn your ideas into money!

Ready for Success 101?

I hope you are ready now to explore Success 101. I am here as your mentor and friend to give you all the tools you need to be successful and to accomplish your dreams.

If you read my first book, then you know that at a very young age, I was struck by a car and left in a coma. When I eventually awoke, half of my body was paralyzed. My brain was injured. Doctors told my mother I would never be able to drive a car and never go to college. But I did not hear those discouraging words. I felt I would be able to overcome *anything.* I did drive a car, did go to college, did get elected (more than once!), because of determination. As time went on, I was determined to succeed—and by my definition and dreams, indeed I have. I recently got married to a wonderful woman—and now I have new dreams and goals.

My co-author, Kevin, too, knows the role that determination plays in a person's success. At thirty-nine, severe pain and loss of dexterity in his left arm and hand revealed a very serious situation with his spinal cord and neck. His doctors gave him two choices. Immediate surgery or risk paralysis for life. After replacing two disks in his neck with titanium and six grueling months of rehabilitation, he saw firsthand how family, faith, determination, and persistence are the keys to overcoming all obstacles.

Overcome obstacles, and success is within your grasp! So now, I am equally determined to pave the way for YOU to succeed as well. No one can stop you. With Success 101, your financial and winning dreams are right there, ready to be fulfilled.

Chapter Three

Saving For Dreams

What is your earliest memory of saving money?

If you are like most people, you probably remember getting a piggybank of some sort. Maybe you saved money in an old tin can or a jar. Maybe you were very little and found some pennies on the ground and your parents told you to put them in your bank. My friend Jack had a ceramic sheep with a coin slot on its back. I had a piggy bank, too, shaped like a superhero.

If you were like me, chances are you picked up your piggy bank once in a while and gave it a good shake! The heavier it was, the more money you knew you had! Maybe you even took the bottom out of the bank and poured all the money out on your bed to count it. I used to play with the coins. Sometimes I looked at them to see the dates. Then I would plug up the bank again and put all the coins back through the slot.

So you probably remember saving.

But what did you save for?

Kevin's parents used to tell him to "save for a rainy day." Other than sounding like you were supposed to save for an umbrella, what does that expression even mean to the average kid? A lot of times, very little kids put money in a piggy bank without really knowing why.

Maybe you even put money in your piggy bank until it was heavy with coins and, though you were saving for a special toy, you opened that bank and spent the money on candy, or ice cream. Did you ever feel guilty because of it? We all know that, as wonderful as candy is, once you eat it, it's gone. Like that! Poof!

Now that you're older, how many times have you been saving for something special—a bike, a new computer, inline skates, whatever—when something more fun came along like a night out at the movies, or a date with the cutest girl or guy in school (come on, you can raise your hand). So you broke into whatever you kept your money in, took it all . . . and spent it! Then you had to start all over again.

And how many of you don't have a place to save your money at all? You don't ever save. The minute you get a paycheck from your part-time job, or cash from your babysitting gig, you run out and spend it—every cent of it. How many of you *never* have money and you're always begging Mom and Dad for an advance against your allowance?

With *Success 101 Dollars and Sense* principles, we're about to change all that.

Why Save?

Reasons for saving are as complex as people. But if you know WHY you want to save, it is easier to be motivated TO save. So before we even talk about HOW to save, we're going to talk about WHY. Saving for a rainy day (in other words, for when times aren't so good, like when you lose a job or an unexpected emergency comes up) is smart. But it's also not too inspiring, is it? Saving for something going wrong is wise, but that's not the stuff dreams are made of. I believe in firing you up, not dampening your dreams. So we're going to instead concentrate on what savings can fund.

* * * * *

 TECH TALK

The PocketMoney app for the iPhone can help you save money by keeping track of any and all bank accounts you have—including tracking where you are spending your money.

http://itunes.apple.com/us/app/
pocketmoney-checkbook-budgets/id283494170?mt=8

* * * * *

If you save, you can fund your dreams, no matter what they are. In order to save big, you need to dream big. Do you want to save to go to Europe for a three-week trip? For college? For a car? For a summer at a special music camp or some other place that will fuel your dreams? For a guitar? Take five minutes right now and come up with six things you would like to save for. Two things should be short-term goals (something smaller like a video game, a pair of sneakers, or your favorite brand of jeans). Two things should be medium-term goals you might have to save for a while to obtain. In this category might be a bicycle, a musical instrument, a mini netbook, or an iPhone or iPod Touch. Finally, two things should be in the long-term goals. That might be paying for college or a car.

Short-term savings goals

1.

2.

Medium-term savings goals

1.

2.

Long-term savings goals

1.

2.

Now we're going to add one more thing. This final item will be important in the next section. Add one "dream big" item. This is something that *right now* you could not imagine having or achieving but deep, deep down you want to achieve it. Maybe it's enough money to travel to Africa for a summer on a safari, or to live in Europe for a semester. Maybe it's a lifelong goal or dream to climb a certain mountain, or see someplace special like Antarctica. Maybe it's a dream of owning your own business or a home. Whatever it is, it should be something that, because of its cost, seems a bit more "impossible." As we will learn, nothing is impossible. List your big dream here:

My big dream is:

Spend some time really *picturing* that big dream. A fairy godmother isn't going to wave a magic wand and make that dream come true. You are responsible for making your dreams come true. And that starts with saving for that dream.

So now we have spent a little time understanding why we save. But does saving really count? Is it worth it?

Does Saving Matter?

First, I'm going to try to blow your mind a little. How would you like to be a millionaire before you are fifty, and all it's going to take is saving $20 a week. For $20 a week, you can have a MILLION dollars when you are fifty years old. But really, if you apply these principles, you will have a lot more.

How?

Simple. A little thing called *compounding interest.*

Compounding interest is one of those amazing "math tricks." It might seem too simple, but it's not. Start using compounding interest *now* and you WILL be a millionaire.

Let's look at the concept.

Let's say that over the next year, you managed to save $100. That seems like a pretty reasonable goal. Between money you get for your birthday, or money from a part-time job or baby-sitting, it seems like that is something the average teenager can accomplish.

* * * * *

TECH TALK

PageOnce is an Android app (or for your iPhone) that helps you save money by keeping track of where you are spending your hard-earned cash, as well as tracking bank accounts, checking accounts, and it offers alerts, like when certain bills are due, or when your savings account gets too low.

http://www.pageonce.com/

* * * * *

Now let's assume you can invest the money some-place that earns you 10 percent interest. (We can go into ways to do that later.) At the end of a year of interest plus the original $100, you would have $110. Now don't touch the money. Leave it there. In the second year, you have $110 earning that inter-est. It compounds (meaning just keep adding it and reinvesting it). That year, you'll earn over $12. If you just keep adding like that, in 50 years (without EVER adding to this account, other than the interest), you will have almost $12,000. Not bad for putting $100 in an account and never touching it again.

But suppose that you managed to save $1,000 for that investment. Maybe your grandparents gave you a large birthday check, and maybe you sold your bike, and you did odd jobs, and at the end of a year, you had $1,000 (which is saving $20 a week). Imagine you never touched that money again, just left it in that same compounding interest account. How much would $1,000 grow to in 50 years? You guessed it ... a nudge over a million dollars.

These examples were based on you *not adding* to your savings account. But suppose, instead, you kept adding to it, and kept earning interest. You added your birthday money. When you got your first job, you set aside 10 percent of your paycheck and added *that* to it. What would happen? Your results could be that much more impressive.

Saving matters. A little bit each week, with the

"magic" of compounding interest, can add up to big financial success.

* * * * *

TECH TALK

No, all that talk about saving isn't hocus-pocus. It's real. Use a simple tool on the Web to see how much YOUR money can grow. At this link, you can list the amount of your principle (what you start with), the interest rate the bank or credit union gives you, and a time frame (one year, two years, five years, etc.) Find out how much you can save!

http://www.fool.com/TEENS/teens13.htm

* * * * *

Saving with Small Sacrifices

Most of the time, people think of saving as physically *doing* something. You work a part-time job, you work as a babysitter, you receive money, you put some of it in savings. For most people:

PAYCHECK = MONEY

And that is true. However, money is also SPENT. You go to the movies ... there goes some of your money. You go shopping for clothes. There it goes again. You go out to eat with your friend—whoops! There goes your money.

And the fact is we all spend money. But being in a "savings" mindset is more than putting money in a bank account. You can look for opportunities to save. Small sacrifices can mean big rewards.

What does that mean? When your favorite movie star's new flick comes out in the theatres and you're dying to see it, you should go right ahead and see the movie and not feel guilty about it. But when the popcorn costs $10 and you KNOW it really costs less than a dollar, do you want those $9 in YOUR pocket or in the movie theater owner's pocket? I don't know about you, but I would like to apply the $10 I might save on soda and popcorn towards my compounding interest "someday I'm going to be a millionaire" account.

Look at some amazing facts:

❖ If you spend $5.00 once a week on a fast food splurge, that's over $250 a year. It's easy to not miss it, but imagine if that money was in your pocket?

❖ Let's say you spend $15 a month on an expensive hairspray, and $15 on an expensive shampoo. And we'll add that once a month, you treat yourself to a manicure for $20. What does that total? A whopping $600 a YEAR!

❖ Buying video games NEW (let's say between $40-$60) versus waiting until you can get them used . . . multiply by how many games you typically buy a year.

I know that part of being a teenager is trying to look your best and also going places with friends, playing video games and indulging in your favorite hobbies. So I don't think you have to give up all the fun stuff. But sit down right now and list five simple "small sacrifices equals big savings" things you could start doing right now.

1.

2.

3.

4.

5.

Once you figure out your monthly savings, start setting that aside for your millionaire fund.

* * * * *

 TECH TALK

Small savings can yield big rewards over time. For example, you can use the Fuel Finder app to find the cheapest gas in your town. If you save money every time you fuel your car, then that adds up over time.

http://itunes.apple.com/us/app/
gas-buddy-cheapest-gas-in/id299969005?mt=8

* * * * *

 **TECH TALK**

Do you *have* to look your best every time you leave the house? Are the latest fashions important to you? Then log onto the Web for the frugal fashionista's tips. Her blog shows you how to duplicate the hottest fashions for budget prices—use the difference in price to put money in your savings account!

http://frugal-fashionista.blogspot.com/

* * * * *

How to Save

Now we're going to get practical. What's the best way to save?

There is a difference between short-term goals and long-term goals and day-to-day expenses.

We all need money to get from day-to-day. (We'll explore that later in budgeting.) Hopefully, with this brief introduction into "Small Sacrifices," you can find ways to spend less money day-to-day. However, whether it is from an allowance, a part-time job, starting your own neighborhood business (mowing lawns, babysitting, washing cars), or gifts at holiday time, you have to figure out a way to divide that money into day-to-day, with a portion set aside for long-term goals and a portion for short-term goals. We will get into percentages later on in budgeting, but for now, create three envelopes.

In envelope #1, put the portion of your money for day-to-day expenses.

In envelope #2, put the portion of money you designate for one of your shorter-term goals (saving for a bike or computer).

In envelope #3, you are going to put money for your bigger dream—whether that's a millionaire fund, a savings account for college, or some other long-term financial goal.

What's more important is this. Envelope #1 should remain accessible to you—but don't make it too easy. You should carry a small amount of cash in your wallet for emergencies, but for things like movies or going out to eat, you should have to pause and think about it before you spend it. Keeping that envelope on the highest shelf in your room, for example, makes it so you can access the cash—but it's not right there on your desk or nightstand where you will be tempted to grab it spontaneously and go and spend.

Envelope #2 should be more inaccessible. That money should go to your parents, for example, with the instructions, "Don't let me have this money unless it's because I have saved enough for the computer I want to purchase." You could also choose a bank branch near your home.

Envelope #3, once you have accumulated enough, should be difficult for you to access. Maybe it's put in a bank with a branch on the other side of town. Or maybe it's in a stock fund called a "money market" that you open, which means you cannot get at your money easily, simply because it is being invested by the fund you choose. Whatever your decision, once money goes in that envelope, try not to access it ever again. It should be earning money for you in an account with compounding interest. (We'll do a little primer on investments later.)

For now, it's enough that you understand the PRINCIPLE of saving. Savings are a "means to an end." I bet you have heard that expression before, but maybe you don't know what it means. Basically, that expression is saying that if you have a dream (college, a computer, being a millionaire), savings are a way to help you achieve it. They are the MEANS to the END (your dream).

But the best part? Dreams aren't really an end.

They are just the beginning.

* * * * *

 TECH TALK

Have a smart phone? *There's an app for that!*
No, really, there are iPhone apps that can help you save.

❖ **Tip & Split – Smart Phone App;** This app lets you enter a restaurant bill total, the number of people, the percentage tip, and it calculates each person's bill.

❖ **Joost – Smart Phone App:** This one is for free TV shows, music, and movies.

❖ **Pocket Money – Smart Phone App**: This is a personal finance manager.

* * * * *

Chapter Four

The Spirit of Giving

In the last chapter, we explored saving for the things we want. But what about giving for the causes we believe in? It might seem that "giving" isn't part of financial dollars and sense, but part of being a successful person isn't how much is in your bank account, but instead who you are as a person. The spirit of giving is very much a part of Success 101. Don't believe me? Let's look at some quotes on giving.

❖ "No person was ever honored for what he received. He was honored for what he gave." ~Calvin Coolidge

❖ "The value of a man resides in what he gives and not in what he is capable of receiving." ~Albert Einstein

❖ "Make all you can, save all you can, give all you can." ~John Wesley

❖ "It is possible to give without loving, but it is impossible to love without giving." ~Richard Braunstein

❖ "He who obtains has little. He who scatters has much."~Lao-Tzu

❖ "You can't have a perfect day without doing something for someone who'll never be able to repay you."~John Wooden

❖ "You can have everything in life that you want if you will just help enough other people get what they want."~Zig Ziglar

❖ "If a person gets his attitude toward money straight, it will help straighten out almost every other area in his life."~Billy Graham

For some, "tithing" is an important part of their religion. When someone tithes, they contribute 10 percent of the money they make to their church. Biblical quotes support this idea and, for some people, that is one reason to be generous. Others have similar concepts for support of a church, synagogue, mosque, temple, or house of worship.

For other people, generosity is about doing the right thing. Most of us would agree that the "Golden Rule" ("Do unto others as you would have them done unto you"—or more basically, treat people the way you want to be treated in return) is a fine principle. Helping those less fortunate is part of that.

However, there are a couple more giving thoughts to explore. As I have toured the country on book tours and speaking engagements, teens and teachers have kindly allowed me into their classrooms to talk to teens directly. Today's teens are more engaged in social issues than ever before. A short list of the things teens care about includes the environment and climate change, AIDS in Africa and around the world, global poverty, mission work on behalf of churches and houses of worship, stopping drunk driving, helping addicts, helping the homeless, supporting our troops, and finding homes for unwanted dogs and cats. In short, you name the cause and kids today are involved with it.

Let me applaud you! Wow! Teens today care. And one way you can show you care about your favorite causes is with your wallet. Teens not only can donate their own money, they can fundraise and find creative measures to raise money for the causes close to them.

Another item I include in this chapter is the idea of "Pocket Power." What's Pocket Power? I made up that phrase to explore the idea that we are each consumers. We spend the money in our pockets on things that are important to us, on items that are necessary (like food and shelter). We spend our pocket money, also, on those things we *want* like tunes for our iPod, clothes, makeup and cosmetics, sports gear, entertainment, and collectibles.

But even as we spend, we can make socially conscious choices. More and more teens are telling me that they are thinking about where they spend their money. For example, some teens choose to buy "Fair Trade" products. "Fair Trade" products invoke a higher environmental and social standard, aimed at helping developing countries. Most often, you will see "Fair Trade" labels on products like chocolate, coffee, fresh fruit, sugar, honey, and handmade goods. When teens buy "Fair Trade" items, they are using Pocket Power to say this is how they are being generous to farmers and workers in poorer or developing nations.

* * * * *

 TECH TALK

http://www.fairtradefederation.org/

The Fair Trade Federation is a great place to start learning about Fair Trade so you can make spending choices that coincide with your beliefs.

* * * * *

 TECH TALK

http://www.teensturninggreen.org/

Teens Turning Green is a national movement of teens transforming the world by investigating and eliminating toxic exposures that threaten our health and the environment.

* * * * *

How else are teens using "Pocket Power"? I've heard from teens who prefer to buy recycled products. They are "thinking green" wherever and whenever they can. This is being generous to the earth and to the next generation.

What Are Your Giving Goals?

Just as you have savings goals, you may have causes and beliefs that you want to support. Why don't you make a list below of causes you feel passionate about?

1.

2.

3.

4.

5.

Don't worry if you don't have five. It's more important that you start thinking of the money you spend and have as possessing a voice, in a way. HOW you spend it says something. WHAT you spend it on says something.

* * * * *

TECH TALK

Have a smart phone? *There's an app for that!*

No, really, there are iPhone apps that can help you live a sustainable life.

Goodguide—Smart Phone App. Want to know about a product you are considering buying? Scan the bar code into this app and it will tell you if it is a safe, healthy, and sustainable product.

* * * * *

Now that you have identified your causes, next to each one list whether it is something you want to contribute to, or something you want to use Pocket Power to "speak" about your commitment—or maybe both!

Now here's the tricky part. Committing to be a giver requires being aware of your spending and buying habits and making clear choices.

For example, a young friend of mine is a committed vegetarian. This cause—not eating meat—is important to her. In addition, she does not like wasteful use of paper products. When she eats out, she makes a choice to go to restaurants that use recycled paper products, and that do not serve meat on the menu. That's not easy in her hometown. That limits her to four restaurants. But she thinks that the Pocket Power of that choice is important.

* * * * *

 TECH TALK

When you give your money to a charity organization, it's important to know how responsible they are with the money you entrust to them. You can visit Charity Navigator, a website that rates charities based on how well they manage their money, and how effectively they get that money to people in need.

http://www.charitynavigator.org

* * * * *

Another friend of mine was in the habit of going to a fast food restaurant on his way home from hockey practice every single weekday. His habit of dropping by his favorite burger joint was costing him, he finally calculated, about $25 a week. However, after hearing a speaker at his church discussing profound poverty in Haiti, he decided to sponsor a child through a charity organization. He suddenly realized he was casually spending $100 a MONTH on fast food—money he could use to give to a cause that moved him. Now he saves the fast food for an occasional treat, and is very excited to know that his money is helping a child in need.

What can *you* do to use your Success 101 principles to make a difference?

Chapter Five

Budgeting the *Success 101* Way

My friend Ann is "directionally-challenged." As she jokes, she "can get lost in a shoebox." She hasn't a clue how to tell north, south, east, and west, even though we live in Florida and I remind her that the ocean is east. So Ann travels everywhere with her GPS in her car.

"I love it!" she tells me. "Now I always know where I am going."

Budgeting your money is like your personal financial GPS. With a budget, you always know where you are going and you won't find yourself detoured by random spending and impulse purchases.

Budgeting 101

Now we're going to walk through a simple budget plan in six easy steps. Set aside an hour of uninterrupted time to create your budget.

1. **Collect all your financial expenses into a list.** Even though you are a teen and aren't likely

to have to pay rent or specific household costs, you may have certain things you are responsible for, such as car insurance or your cell phone bill. Financial expenses aren't purchases or entertainment. Instead, these are the things you are expected to pay every month. Depending on your family, this total might be zero—or it could be significant if you have to pay your own way for certain items.

2.   List all your income. For teens, this number can fluctuate quite a bit. Most teens I know babysit or pick up work mowing lawns or helping with extra chores. The best way to handle fluctuating income is to look at three months and come up with an average. If you have a steady part-time job and if you get an allowance, those figures will likely be fixed, but if you pick up work doing pet-sitting, or seasonal work during the holidays of some sort, then an average will help you get an idea over the course of a year.

3.   List your monthly expenses. This is where you list all your expenses. Your expenses can be: car payments, car insurance payments, cell phone expenses, a college fund where you put money every month, entertainment, food/dining out, dry cleaning, clothing, haircuts, beauty products, sports/team fees, sport uniforms, etc. Sometimes, this category can be surprising. You might not realize just how much money you spend! If you have a tough time with this category, take a pocket notebook (or use the notepad on a smartphone, if you have one) and keep track of *every single penny* you spend for the next week or two. Every single penny. Are you spending $2 a day buying soda from a machine? You could buy a six-pack at the store and spend a fraction of what you are paying for convenience. Did you not realize that your fancy coffees *really* cost $4.50 each? Track *every penny* and find out where your money is going and remember, your budget is like a GPS system for your money.

4. Add up your income and expenses separately. This is the moment of truth. Do you have more expenses than income? The numbers don't lie. It can be ugly, but the thing about financial success is you can't be successful by *hiding from the truth.* You must really and truly know where you stand, even if the numbers make you cringe a little bit.

5. Tweak your budget. Ideally, you want to have more income than expenses—or more accurately, you want them to be the same. Since we have already covered saving money, any "extra" income is already going toward savings—both long-term savings and short-term savings. But what if you have more expenses than income?

You're going to tweak your budget. You'll learn how in the next section.

6. Look at your budget weekly. Once you have a working budget, don't just stick it in a drawer and forget about it. USE IT! Like your GPS, it's a map for where you are going financially. Review your budget every week or at least every other week to make sure you are staying on track.

* * * * *

 TECH TALK

Have a Mac or an iPhone? Cha-ching can help you track your budget on the go!

http://www.macupdate.com/app/mac/22913/cha-ching

Have a PC and want something free to do the tracking? You can download these free Excel templates to track your budget.

http://office.microsoft.com/en-us/templates/personal-budget-worksheet-TC006206279.aspx

* * * * *

Tweaking Your Budget

All right, you now have the not-so-good news that you are spending more money than you are taking in . . . or you have no money left over to save for college or a car or other big purchase. What do you do now?

You tweak your budget.

Here's how in three easy steps.

   1. **Examine your income.** The simple fact is that if your budget doesn't balance, you need to either add more income or take away some expenses. There's no way around it. First, examine your income. While you don't want your schoolwork to suffer, is there a way to add a couple of hours a week to your part-time job? Or can you start a small neighborhood business— babysitting, petsitting, dog walking, car washing, lawn mowing? Do you have a special talent that you can use to make money? My friend's daughter has been playing violin since she was four years old. By the time she was in high school, she was making $150 an HOUR as a violinist in a chamber music wedding quartet. Maybe you can paint murals, or teach younger children how to make jewelry. Whatever your talent, chances

are, if you are good enough at it, you can use it to make money.

2. Examine your expenses. Go through your expense list again. Place a checkmark next to the expenses that aren't *fixed. Fixed* expenses are the expenses that you have to pay no matter what. For example, if you pay for your own car insurance or you pay your own cellphone bill, you can't cut those expenses unless you give up driving or give up your phone (which you can do, but it's not likely). *Variable* expenses are those expenses that *aren't* fixed. In other words, they can be tweaked. For now, just put a checkmark.

3. Trim your expenses. Now look at your checkmarked items. How can you trim your expenses? Where are you spending money you don't need to? Can you cut out fast food meals? What about sodas bought on the run instead of from home? Do you *need* a new pair of sneakers every other month? Can you cut your hair every eight weeks instead of every six weeks? Look at *every single checkmarked item.* Is it a *need* or a *want*? Most, I am betting, are "wants." And that means you can figure out some way to trim. I'm not saying you have to give up your weekly Friday night movies. But maybe don't buy the $5 box of candy each time.

* * * * *

 TECH TALK

Like working on the computer? This free software at Mint.com can help you store your budget and manage your personal budgeting goals with the click of a keyboard. Attractive charts and graphs mean it's easy to understand—and fun, too!

http://www.mint.com/

* * * * *

Remember Your Savings Goals to Help Trim Impulsive Spending

Remember those big savings goals you established? Create some tangible sign of them. Cut out a picture of the Macbook you want or the car you are saving for. If it's a trip to Europe or some great sports camp, cut out pictures of that. If it's your dream college, clip a picture of the mascot or a picture of the campus. Tape your savings goals somewhere you will see often, like your bathroom mirror. Then you won't be so tempted to cheat on your budget or to go back to your old spending habits. Once you've tweaked and trimmed your budget, you will get used to it. Especially if you remember the big picture.

Chapter Six

Your Financial Plan

Many adults turn to a "Certified Financial Planner" when it comes to establishing a financial plan for themselves. A financial plan is that "big picture." It's taking what you have learned so far in this book and coming up with a plan for the future. All the things you have learned so far are pieces. Now it's time to take the pieces and create a puzzle picture.

Your financial plan has four steps.

Financial Planning 101

1. **Where are you now?** You need to determine your financial picture right now. Your budget probably helped you look at where you are with your spending, but the bigger financial picture also includes savings, a checking account if you have one, and longer-term savings (such as if you have savings bonds or stocks set aside by a grandparent or parent for when you go to college).

2. **Where you going?** We all need goals. You

have goals for what you are saving, but a financial plan aims at your short and long-range financial picture. People do not have ONE financial planning goal. They have several. You want to have a financial planning goal for one year from today, two years from today, four years from today, and seven years from today. The reason I am asking you to do that is teen's lives change—and they change in a hurry. Some of you reading this will be graduated from college in a few years. What are your financial planning goals for that time in your life? For example, let's write out four sample financial planning goals.

"In one year, I want to have $500 saved up in my college fund and have no debt by paying my parents back for any money I have borrowed."

"In two years, I want to have $1,200 in my savings account, and I want to have paid off my car."

"In four years, while I am in college, I want to maintain $1,500 in my saving account and be able to pay for all my books without dipping into that money."

"In seven years, I want to graduate from college and have $4,000 saved toward a first

apartment, and have a job that is paying for my student loans.

3. What's your plan? Like driving a car with that GPS we talked about, a plan is how you are going to get from point A to point B. Too many self-help books out there can give the impression that it's enough to visualize your goals or enough to just write them down. It's not. Every goal should come with a plan for how you are going to achieve it. Start with your smaller financial planning goals. If your plan is to save $500, then you need to return to the budget you prepared and examine it. Is there room in your budget for you to save $500 if you plan carefully? If there isn't, then it isn't possible to achieve your goal. Does that mean you should abandon your financial planning goal? No! If the goal is *realistic* (in other words, if it does not require you winning the lottery!), then you can return to your budget and tweak it again (remember, you should be looking at your budget every week or two) so that you *can* achieve the goals you have set. You should follow suit with your remaining financial goals. As you look two years ahead or longer, something to keep in mind is that at certain times of the year, your "earning potential" can go way up. I'm talking about summer! So you might write your plan in such a way to include

"Get a part-time job working a minimum of 20 hours a week each summer."

4. Work your plan! Okay, so you're almost there. Now that you HAVE a financial plan, you have to WORK your financial plan. This means having a weekly or biweekly meeting with yourself to assess how you are doing. If you let weeks go by, blow your budget, lose sight of your plan, that is just a step away from abandoning your plan and "winging it." Remember your GPS and you will arrive at your destination.

* * * * *

But What About the Economy?

At the time of this writing, the United States is going through a very tough time economically. So is Europe and most of the globe. These can be scary times. Worse, some teens and college students (and adults!) can feel like *why make plans when I won't be able to find a job?* I will be the first to admit that these are difficult times. But there is a tried and true principle I believe in. *When the going gets tough, the tough get going.*

For example, you might feel like the idea of college or trade school is pointless. After all, you could graduate and not be able to find a job. But the fact is, sooner or later, things will turn around and those with a degree or skill will be in better shape than those without a degree or skill.

Another point to make is that you might *not* be able to find a part-time job. Unfortunately, in these economic times, some of the part-time jobs that teens used to have no longer exist—or they are being given to out-of-work adults. For example, the people who *used* to deliver my pizza were college students. Now, often, when I answer the door, I see adults who are well-groomed and well-spoken, and I am assuming laid-off from a former position. They need the part-time work to get them through these tough times.

However, you can still *create* your own job. We'll discuss that in the chapter on entrepreneurship. But again, if you can walk dogs, or play music at a wedding, or sell crafts ... you can still make money in this economy. It's important not to be discouraged or give up.

* * * * *

Chapter Seven

Learning

If you read the first Success 101 book or saw me on television, then you know I am a firm believer in education. Everyone can pursue education. It might be college, a trade school, a course in computer programming, or beauty school, but everyone in this country can go on to better themselves through knowledge.

The recent financial crisis in our country, though, has made it abundantly clear that people need a basic financial education. I wanted to explain a few general financial principles here, and then we have included a glossary in the back of the book for other terminology.

Bank Accounts

First, do you have your own bank accounts? Most banks offer what they call "student accounts," which means they do not charge you any fees for having your accounts at the bank. It is important that you ask about this since some banks charge a service fee each month, particularly if your account balance is below a certain point.

A **checking account** allows you to write a check against the money you hold in the account. If, for example, you have $100 in your checking account, you could write a check for $100 that the checkholder could then cash at the bank.

The tricky thing with a checking account is you must always keep track of your **balance.** If you, for example, log in online and check how much money is in your account, and it says $100, but you wrote a check for $20—and forgot to write it down in your balance book, and then wrote a check for $90, your check would **bounce.** That means that you have insufficient funds for the amount of checks you have written. You thought you had the $90, but you really only had $80. If both checks went through the bank for processing at the same time, you would be penalized by both the bank and the other person's bank.

Sometimes checking accounts can earn **interest.** Interest is a percentage paid to you for the bank getting the use of your money, in effect. It can also be interest *you* pay for money you are loaned—like for a student loan. When you are the one loaning the money (which, in effect, you do by storing your money in a bank), you want the highest percentage you can get. When you are the one borrowing the money (more on this later in the chapter), you want the lowest percentage you can get.

* * * * *

TECH TALK

http://www.bls.gov/k12/

It's never too early to be thinking about your future. This site offers all kinds of resources to explore education and career ideas.

* * * * *

Savings accounts are interest-earning accounts in which you save money. Most student accounts do not have minimum balance requirements. Some types of savings accounts are called **money market** accounts. These can be offered by banks or credit unions. Money market accounts generally earn higher interest (good for you, the saver). However, they might require $1000 to start one. Also, you might be limited to just three withdrawals a month (this will depend on the bank). Considering you are trying to build your savings, that will hopefully not matter.

The Basics of Interest

Interest is a fee paid for using someone else's money. If you are a borrower, you pay interest. If you are the lender, you earn interest.

There are two types of interest. **Simple interest** is straightforward. With simple interest, if you put $100 in a savings account and earned 5% interest on that money, at the end of the year, you would have $105 if you didn't take out any money from your account or add any money into it.

Compounding interest we covered earlier. With compounding interest, if you are the borrower (on a loan), you will pay ever-increasing amounts for the same basic sum you borrowed. And, if you remember when we talked about savings with compound interest, it is a way to continually multiply your interest and your savings.

Debt *Don'ts*

Two important things to keep in mind regarding borrowing money is debt—and your credit score.

Credit cards are a part of life for most of America. They allow for quick purchases. They are convenient. In some cases, you can earn points toward things like airline tickets, or you can earn cash back. The problem arises when you do not pay the WHOLE balance off each and every month. By carrying some of your debt over to the next month, you pay interest. Unfortunately, unlike interest you might earn on your own money in a savings account (let's say 3.5%), you can pay as high as 22% or more for credit card interest. If you miss a payment, or it arrives late, you will pay a penalty AND that high interest rate. In fact, your credit card company could raise your interest rate just because you were late with one payment.

If you fall in the habit of spending for purchases on your credit card and ONLY paying the minimum amount, you could take ten years or longer to pay off a single large purchase—all that time paying interest. So if you bought a computer for $1000, over time, adding other purchases on, etc., your computer could ACTUALLY cost you $5000 or more. It simply isn't worth it.

However, one good thing credit cards can do for you is help you to establish a credit history. This is important when you go to buy a car or rent your first apartment. Your credit history tells lenders whether you are a good risk or a bad risk for paying back the money you owe them or for paying your bills on time.

A big mistake you can make is ignoring your credit history. In today's times of doing so much online, identity theft is a real problem. You could find you have a poor score and you've never even used credit! Or, be like a friend of mine, who discovered that medical bills she thought her insurance company paid actually were not—and her score was lower.

Putting It All Together

As you can see, being educated about finances is important. Each component of this book, from saving money, to balancing a checkbook, to avoiding debt, is part of the Dollars and Sense of Success 101.

Chapter Eight

Entrepreneurship and Careers

I remember what it was like to be a teenager. Sometimes, you just want to grow up faster. But sometimes, it would be nice to stay young forever. Getting older means responsibilities.

Have you thought about what you might want to "be when you grow up"? Do you hate that question? Part of dreaming for the future is making sure you can have a career of some sort.

* * * * *

 TECH TALK

You can log onto this websites to take a test that can help you see what careers might suit you.

http://www.careerpath.com/

http://www.quizrocket.com/career-quiz

* * * * *

Though I have written about saving for college, there are all sorts of options for you. Technical training can teach you a job skill—like repairing cars or refrigerators or computers—that will be valuable on a career path.

What are your likes? Dislikes? Interests?

Though it is important to have a career, I want to say something very important. Getting up every day to go to work at a job you hate can feel like a prison sentence. I have a friend who went to work for a bank, even though she didn't find banking very interesting. Worse, she worked for a "toxic" boss. In other words, just as there are bullies in middle school and high school, there are bully bosses. And this boss was one. She was awful—negative, hurtful in all her comments, playing favorites in the office, bending the rules in ways that were borderline illegal and so on. After a while, my friend changed. She was a nervous wreck and never knew when her boss would lash out with ugly language. She was unhappy. When weekends came, all she did was sleep. Eventually, the bank had financial difficulties and there were layoffs and then a closure. Getting fired, my friend said, was the BEST thing that ever happened to her. She went on to find a job she loved—one she still has to this day. And though every day isn't perfect, overall, she feels blessed.

Having a job is important, but having one you love can make it not *seem* like a job. There are vocations. And there are avocations. Vocations are jobs/careers.

Avocations are usually thought of as hobbies—things you love to do. But some people turn avocations into vocations. For example, the comic book collector who starts a successful eBay shop to sell comic books to other collectors. Or the pet lover who starts a pet sitting business—or invents a new type of pet treat or toy and sells it.

Entrepreneurship is the idea of working for yourself. Some people will always want the steady income of a paycheck and working for someone else. There's nothing wrong with that. Other people treasure the idea of creating their own business.

You may have goals, long-term, for having your own business. And there are businesses you can start NOW. Here are some ideas.

Designing Web sites. Turn your skills with HTML, Flash, or other Web design programs into money. You can earn $50/hour or more designing Web sites for local companies. Put a smile on your face and walk into new shops or retailers, doctors' practices, or other places of business in your hometown and tell them about your services. Design a simple brochure. Dress professionally. Show them a web site you designed (even if it's the one for your own services!).

* * * * *

 **TECH TALK**

http://careerinfonet.com/

America's Career InfoNet helps people make better, more informed career decisions. You can learn about education, knowledge, skills, and abilities, and licensing requirements for certain kinds of jobs.

* * * * *

❖ **Social Media.** Do you like to Tweet? Live on Facebook? Why not turn your online skills into work doing social media for local companies. They can pay you a set fee per week for you to go online and tweet their business specials, find new "friends," and so on.

❖ **Computer repair and training.** I have a friend whose father (in his late 70s) wants to learn the computer. But she has no time to train him. That's where you can come in. Use your computer know-how to train senior citizens or computer newbies. Or install anti-viral software and programs, and generally repair glitches.

❖ **Lawn mowing and lawn care.** Work in the summer and after school. A little muscle work, and a few regular clients and you will be earning money in no time.

❖ **Babysitting.** Take a class in infant CPR and First Aid to show prospective parents/ clients how serious you are about doing a good job. Arrive with crafts and crayons and story-books. Go above and beyond what a "typical" babysitter might do and you'll be raking in the cash in no time.

❖ **Sell online.** With sites like Etsy and eBay, everyone can be an online entrepreneur. You can sell crafts, collectibles, and frequent flea markets for stuff to sell. One young friend of mine started a business in which he went to people's homes and offered to clean their garages and attics, and find stuff to sell. He then set up an online shop, sold these attic treasures and split the "finds" 50/50 with the client. They got a clean garage or attic. He got profits.

* * * * *

TECH TALK

http://www.kidsmoney.org

This is a general financial education resource for Teens, Kids, Parents, and Teachers. Now that you're a financial expert, you can share with mom and dad and your siblings and friends, too!

* * * * *

Glossary

Activity

When you open an account at a bank—checking or savings—*activity* is when anything changes. Interest is added, withdrawals, deposits. These are all activities.

Amortized Loan

This is an installment loan that is paid off in multiple equal payments. For example, if you buy a car, your monthly payment might be, for example, $220 every month for four years.

Annual Percentage Rate

APR is the interest rate the bank pays over one year for savings accounts. It also means the percentage rate *you* pay over one year for credit cards or other loans.

Balance

Balance can be one of two things. If you have a checking account or a savings account, for example, your *balance* is the total amount of money in there, including interest and the principle.

If you have a credit card account, your *balance* is really the "balance due"—meaning the money you still have to pay—including interest.

Bounced Check

This is something you *don't* want to have. If you write a check to someone but somehow miscalculated how much money was in your account, the bank will "bounce" your check. They will return the check to the person and tell them you didn't have enough money to cover the amount. Not only is this embarrassing, your bank will charge you a fee (maybe $30 for ONE check). Then the *other* person's bank or company could charge you a fee, and that could be $50 for ONE check! That is one expensive mistake!

Budget

This is the plan you create of how much to spend and what you will spend on. There will be fixed items—items you have to pay—and then variable items, like entertainment, that you don't HAVE to pay, but are more "wants."

Compound Interest

If you set aside money in a bank account with compounding interest, it is interest that is paid on the principal and any interest earned so far. It keeps multiplying based on always adding that interest to the principal.

Fixed Costs

When we explored budgeting we discussed fixed costs and variable costs. Fixed costs are regular, ongoing costs that don't go away, like your cell phone bill every month. They must be paid.

Entrepreneur

Someone who starts his or her own business.

Principal

With a loan, it is the amount of money you owe. In a savings account, it is the amount of the original deposit you put in there, not the interest.

Principle

Principles are rules to live by.

Simple Interest

This is interest that is paid on the principal only.

Tithe

Giving 10 percent, or a first part of your income, to charity, which can be a church, synagogue, house of worship, or the charity of your choice.

Variable Costs

These are costs that vary or change. When you did your budget, they were the costs with a checkmark next to them, meaning they could be "tweaked"— changed—because they were wants more than needs, most of the time.

Part II

Your Financial Success Plan

What are your short-term savings goals?

1.

2.

What are your medium-term savings goals?

1.

2.

What are your long-term savings goals?

1.

2.

Dream Big

My big dream is:

Now have some fun. Use the space below to make a "vision page"—make your dream more real. Cut out pictures from magazines, or sketch something about your dream. You could also write words that remind you of your big dream. Keep this near you and look at it often to discourage you from impulse spending.

What are your spending weaknesses?

List five things that you spend money on that, when looking at your big dream, you could perhaps bypass and save the money instead.

My weaknesses are:

1.

2.

3.

4.

5.

Your Budget

For one week, write down EVERY PENNY you spend.

Monday

Tuesday

Wednesday

Thursday

Friday

Saturday

Sunday

Budget: Income

If you have a regular part-time job, take three pay-checks, add them together and divide by three to get your average weekly income.

If you have varied income, like babysitting, total your income for four weeks and divide by four to get a rough average.

Budget: Are you in the black or in the red?

Do you have more income than expenses?

If not, you must play with your budget.

If you have more income than expenses—but are not able to save very much, then you must play with your budget.

Budget: Where can you cut?

Go back to your expenses and put a checkmark next to EVERY expense that you could cut, for example, if you buy fancy coffee drinks rather than drinking coffee brewed at home and taking a to-go mug.

For two weeks, cut those expenses and put the money you save in an envelope for a savings account. How much were you able to save?

Inspired? Go BACK to your budget and see what else you can cut. Do the same thing.

How much money did you save this month?

Budget: Increasing Your Income

Besides cutting expenses, you could raise your income.

Brainstorm here for ideas for earning income.

Go through the list you created and choose three ideas to explore further.

Use this space to create a financial mission statement using your Success 101 Principles.

About the Authors

MARK HANSEN relates to teens' struggles in adolescence because he struggled through tough events in his own life. As a child, Mark was hit by a car while riding his bike. This put him in a coma for the next eight days, paralyzed him on the left side of his body, and caused seizures for the next nine years. Mark had to learn how to walk and talk again. His mother was told by a psychologist that he would never be college material. He was also told by his doctor that he would never be able to drive a car. Mark was on medication for nine years and always was teased by students. Mark now is not only a successful businessman in real estate, but he is a former elected official who served two terms on the Palm Beach County School Board, the 11th largest school district in the country. He has also authored two previous books, *An Ark for Learning* and *Success 101 for Teens: 7 Traits for a Winning Life*. Mark is a graduate of Florida Atlantic University with a degree in communications.

Mark Hansen has an extensive entrepreneurial background with his first speech given back in 1991 to a group of middle school students. Since then, he has given over 1,500 seminars, and appeared on radio and television programs. In addition, Mark has been a real estate professional for the last 16 years and ranks consistently in the top 3 percent nationally.

Mark has received numerous awards which include the Nido Qubein Scholarship Award from the National Speakers Association and the Dorothy Finkelhor Award from the Florida Speakers Association. He was inducted into the National Society for Collegiate Scholars at Florida Atlantic University, and Mark has won the Excellence in Education award from Northwood University. In 2012, he received the Palm Beach State College Martin Luther King Leadership Award.

Mark is enthusiastic and is driven to make the world a better place. Mark's accomplishments are an example of what can be done even in the face of adversity. Mark lives in Parkland, Florida, with his wife Jane.

KEVIN S. FERBER is a Senior Solution Director for Managed Services with Oracle Corporation. He is responsible for identifying and deploying the best business practices used across the enterprise, with a focus on delivering measurable value to Oracle clients.

Before joining Oracle, he spent more than seven years with Electronic Data Systems (EDS), consulting with Fortune 1000 companies within IT, business operations, and data management.

He holds a bachelor's degree in business management from the University of Miami, a master's of business administration degree from Nova University, a master's degree in marketing/sales from

Nova Southeastern University and has completed his doctoral course work in Finance with Nova Southeastern University. Over the last 20 years, he has shared his knowledge and expertise by lecturing around the world for colleges and universities—including Embry Riddle Aeronautical University, Dowling College, Nova Southeastern, and American Continental University—in technology, economics, finance, marketing and general business courses. He is a frequent speaker for many organizations on technology trends, business strategy, and transformation in the Southeast.

Kevin has devoted over 30,000 hours to study, research, lecture, and writing on education, values, and character traits for youths. He co-founded An Ark for Learning, a non-profit foundation set up to focus on Character Education and Development for youth, as well as the Pay it Forward Program for Education and Cancer Research. Kevin lives in Parkland, Florida, with his wife Pamela and their two children, Kelly Sarah and Kenneth Sean.